ABC Eat Local WISCONSIN

Written by:
Rebekah Johnson

Illustrated by:
Karl Kralapp

Published by Orange Hat Publishing 2020
ISBN 978-1-64538-138-9

Copyrighted © 2020 by Rebekah Johnson
All Rights Reserved
ABC Eat Local Wisconsin
Written by Rebekah Johnson
Illustrated by Karl Kralapp

All Rights Reserved. Written permission must be secured from the publisher to use or reproduce any part of this book, except for brief quotations in critical reviews or articles.

For information, please contact:

Orange Hat Publishing
www.orangehatpublishing.com
Waukesha, WI

The first thing to know about these ABCs
Is we're more than just apples and bratwurst and cheese.
We wrote a few verses so we could play host
And we hope you don't mind if we show off and boast.
We really just want you to know
All the foods that we cook, bake, and grow!

A is for
ASPARAGUS

A mighty big affair for us,
The surest sign that spring is really here.
Those green shoots in a row
Means finally, no snow!
It won't be long 'til strawberries appear!

C is for

CHERRY

Its seasons do vary.
In summer you must be alert,
For one week they're many
The next only twenty.
Make jam or a yummy dessert!

D is for
DAIRY

Those cows on the prairie
They bring us our state's pride and joy
Cheese, milk, and butter
All come from an udder
A fine substitution for soy!

E is for EGG

And you won't have to beg.
Most hens will produce one per day.
If they roam in the open
When their shells are broken,
"This egg is so good!" you will say.

F is for
FORAGE

The woods are a storage
For so many things you can eat.
Be careful, it's tricky!
So be really picky!
If you're not real sure, then retreat!

G is for
GARLIC

And here's a bizarre trick:
It helps when you're not feeling well.
If you eat it, we're told
You can ward off a cold
But watch out for that garlicky smell!

H is for HONEY

But you know what's so funny?
You may be a bit scared of bees.
They make this sweet magic
So it would be tragic
If you didn't say thank you and please.

I is for
ICE CREAM

And here there's a nice theme.
Just add eggs, and voilà! It's custard!
It's rich and delightful
But it would be frightful
To eat with a dollop of mustard!

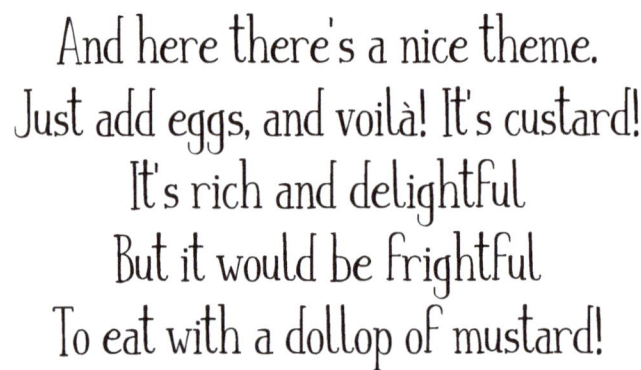

J is for
JELLY

So good in your belly.
We make it to save up the summer.
When the berries arrive
Grab a jar, maybe five!
A nice gift for your teacher or plumber!

K is for
KRINGLE

It's part of this jingle.
Even though kale is good
If we feature one "K"
This one might make your day.
Try almond! Try cherry! You should!

L is for
LEEK

Which is long, green, and sleek.
It's best in the months close to fall.
In soup or sautéed
A nice meal you've made.
It's a leek! It's unique after all!

M is for
MAPLE

It's truly a staple.
In March it comes out of the trees.
On pancakes it goes
So just follow your nose
To the sweet scent of spring on the breeze.

N is for
NACHOS

But you have to watch those!
You can't eat this snack every day.
In fall we love football,
It's always a good call
To pass some around on a tray.

O is for
OKRA

Did we mention polka?
A vegetable, and our state dance.
This rhyme we created
Are things unrelated
But try both! Go on! Take a chance!

P is for
PARSNIP

When temps take a sharp dip,
This root is okay with less sun.
Roasted or mashed
You'll be glad these are stashed
In the ground after summer is done.

Q is for
QUACK

Hey, cut us some slack!
We can't think of anything better.
It's the sound that ducks make
When they're out on the lake
Let's move on, past this challenging letter!

R is for
RHUBARB

It grows in your backyard
Year after year without trouble.
With berries you pair it,
We think you should share it
You probably should've made double!

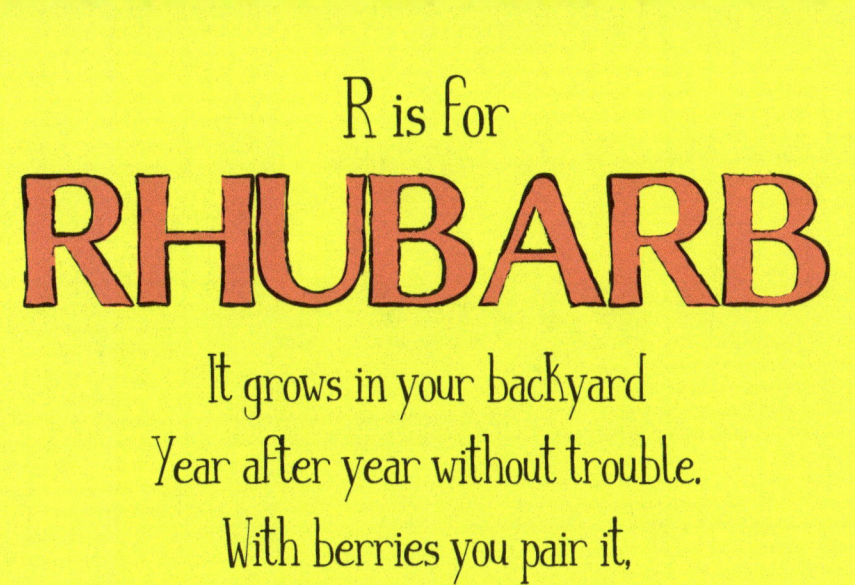

S is for
SQUASH

It's so good, oh my gosh!
It comes when the leaves start to change.
There are so many kinds
That it boggles our minds
To not try them all would be strange!

T is for
TOMATO

Grow some if you're able.
It's easy and we think that you should try.
And when they're good and ready
We're thinking of spaghetti.
Let's make a never-ending sauce supply!

U is for

UDDER

Without it, we shudder!
Our state has a cheese fascination.
We're so fond of the cow,
We should say, "Take a bow!"
Let's give them a standing ovation!

V is for
VEGETABLE

We think it's incredible
How many this state can stock.
The winter is long
But when the snow's gone
Then off to the market we flock.

W is for
WALLEYE

And if you can't recall why
Just look at all the lakes around the state.
In summer we sure wish
That we could fish and fish!
What's that? You want to come? Then it's a date!

X is for
XYLOPHONE

Our theme's been overthrown.

This one is not even food!

But leaving "x" out

Is like brats with no kraut

And wouldn't that be kind of rude?

Y is for
YAM

Oh yes, sir, oh yes, ma'am!
You'll find them at Thanksgiving dinner.
But to stop there is wrong
For they grow all year long
In Wisconsin, that makes them a winner!

Z is for
ZUCCHINI

It's good in fettucine
Or slice it up and eat it in a salad.
All summer it's abundant.
We're done, we feel triumphant!
One more verse should do to end this ballad.

The ABCs of local food
Is something we must now conclude
Even though there may be some we missed.
With an extra alphabet
There's still a few we might forget!
Our state is rich with food, it's quite a list!

www.ingramcontent.com/pod-product-compliance
Lightning Source LLC
Chambersburg PA
CBHW041637040426
42449CB00021B/3489